HEAVEN and HELL

Children's Visions of
HEAVEN
and HELL

Innocent Observations on the Afterlife

Compiled by TIMOTHY FREKE

TRIUMPH™ BOOKS
Liguori, Missouri

Published by Triumph™ Books
Liguori, Missouri 63057-9999
An Imprint of Liguori Publications

First published in Great Britain 1997 by Godsfield Press
Hampshire, United Kingdom

All rights reserved. No part of this publication may be reproduced, stored in a retrieval system, or transmitted in any form or by any means—electronic, mechanical, photocopy, recording, or any other—except for brief quotations in printed reviews without the prior permission of the publisher.

Library of Congress Cataloging-in-Publication Data

Children's visions of heaven and hell: innocent observations on the afterlife/compiled by Timothy Freke. – 1st ed.
    p. cm.
   ISBN 0-7648-0089-2 (alk. paper)
   1. Future life—Miscellanea. 2. Children—Religious life.
I. Freke, Timothy, 1959–
BL535.C53 1997
291.2'3—dc20   96-35820
                            CIP

Copyright © 1997 Godsfield Press
Text compilation © 1997 Timothy Freke
Printed in Singapore
97 98 99 00 01 5 4 3 2 1
First U.S. Edition

This book is dedicated to little Beau and his wonderful mum Debbie.

Acknowledgements

I would like to express my appreciation to Neil Vasey, whose skilled and sensitive facilitating of Circle Time brought out from the young participants their imaginative contributions. I would also like to thank all the children who took part – it is, above all, their book.

Contents

Circle Time
page 6

Heaven
page 10

Hell
page 38

Circle Time

THE CHILDREN WHO shared their insights and pictures to create this little book are between six and nine years old. Most of the material was gathered using an innovative technique, inspired by traditional Native American practises, called children's "Circle Time." In Circle Time a relaxed environment of mutual respect is created that enables the children to feel free to communicate without inhibitions. It allows an adult to help the children to share their thoughts, without interfering or shaping them in any way. As the name suggests, the participants form a circle so that no one is at the front (not even the adult) and no one is at the back. Everyone is an equal part of the circle, like the spokes of a wheel. Just like the children on the beach in William Golding's *Lord of the Flies*, the children in Circle Time pass round a conch shell or some other symbolic, tactile object. Only the child who holds the conch is allowed to speak, and everyone else is expected to listen attentively. A child who does not wish to speak may simply say "pass" and give the conch to his or her neighbor.

When I first sat in on a Circle Time the children themselves explained the "rules" to me. Everyone could say whatever they wished, but they should not put anyone else down – not with words, or by laughing, or with horrible looks, or by embarrassing them. They should not name another child – if they wanted to complain at being pushed around in the playground, for example, they would say "someone is bullying me" without naming the particular child in front of the group. They are encouraged to return home and discuss the contents of Circle Time with their families, but should not ascribe a comment to anyone, because everything said in Circle Time is confidential – although the adult makes it clear to the children that this does not include anything they may say that suggests they are in any danger.

At the beginning of Circle Time each child takes the conch and says how he or she feels today – "happy," "bored," "excited," "tired," and so on. Children who are miserable may be made "special people" by asking them if they would like to sit in the center of the circle while everyone says something nice about them. Such building of self-esteem and mutual support is also encouraged by sharing "Golden Coins." The children can give a "Golden Coin" by saying something positive about another child – and they get two back in return.

Circle Time can also be used to promote gentle physical contact, using simple techniques like asking the children to stand up and gently tap the shoulders of the child in front. In such ways, social skills are developed and bad behavior like bullying is addressed constructively. Under the guidance of a sensitive adult, Circle Time is a simple and playful discipline that creates a safe and supportive space, bringing out of the children the type of wonderful observations that comprise this book.

Heaven

ONE THING IS CLEAR, in Heaven children believe "you can do what you want and run about" and "no one bosses you about," whilst in Hell "you are made to stay still" and "someone follows you around all the time." Their visions are not all such homely reflections of their present experience of childhood, however. Paul imagines souls lifting up into the air and becoming stars – spontaneously rediscovering a myth of the ancient Egyptians. Tom sees Heaven as populated by flying horses, as did the ancient Celts. Like the ancient Greeks, Laura thinks we visit Heaven when we sleep. David thinks Heaven is everywhere but we can't see it – the ultimate teaching of mystical traditions all over the world. The children show a moving sensitivity to the sufferings of others. Lewis would like the homeless to get an extra fifty

11

years in Heaven as compensation for their lack of happiness here on earth, and Emma thinks Heaven is sad as well as happy, because we will look down and see people crying about our death. A number of children suggest that after Heaven a soul is reborn on earth – the doctrine of reincarnation found amongst Hindus, Buddhists, and many others. All these innocent but insightful observations give us glimpses into the inner lives of children who have, if the reincarnationists amongst them are to be believed, not long left the heavenly realms.

You can play games
and meet all your family
and friends there,
but you never sleep.
You eat nice things in Heaven
and you always get what you want
and if you want
something changed,
then you get it changed.

Tracey

If you are good you go
up to Heaven and God
is really nice.

Laura

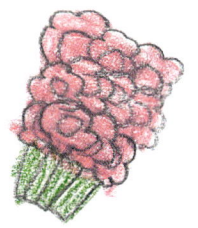

In Heaven there won't
be no burglaries.

Nathan

I know some people in Heaven. I'm glad they are in Heaven, but I wish they were here.

Jenny

In Heaven there will be your relatives, so it will be nice to go up there when you die.

Cassie

The souls go to God's house.
I used to think it was a sort of church.
I still do believe they go to somewhere
like the Empire State Building, except much
older and made of a lot of rocks.
It looks like a pentagon or a hexagon.
It looks like a church.

Nickie

You see God there.
You can do what you want to do.
And the weather is nice.

Kirstie

In Heaven there will be
no one to boss you about.

James

I think you are free to go
anywhere and no one bosses
you about.

Sarah

My Grandma is in Heaven
and I wish I could visit her for a holiday
because when she went away
she didn't say goodbye.

Dean

Angels are in Heaven, because some babies die and they will have to go to Heaven, and there's no one to look after them, so the angels can look after them.

Louise

In Heaven everyone has lots of money.

George

In Heaven you will meet all of your friends and family and pets.

Sam

Heaven is a good place where good people go. It is quiet and peaceful

Heaven is light.

Ashley

When someone dies they probably go up in the sky.
A long way up, to a dark place in space.
It looks really dark and sometimes it gets cold
and sometimes light, because of the sun.
Astronauts go there. Millions of people who have
been astronauts have been there.

Nickie

In Heaven it never gets dark. Heaven is full of flowers.

Peter

I think Heaven is nice and peaceful, and everyone is friendly to you.

Thomas

Heaven is just like home, but a bit nicer.

Laura

Heaven is a nice place
with angels that help you
and you can't get hurt.
And if you're hungry
you suddenly don't feel
hungry again.

John

Angels can fly
just by thinking about it.
I'd like to be an angel.

Angela

Heaven is a peaceful place
Everyone is happy and nice
to each other.

Danielle

I think you can go back and put the things that you did wrong right. I think it's everywhere, but you can't see it. It's brilliant.

David

You can look down on your family and see what they are doing.

Laura

Some people say God has a beard, but I think he is a big, big eye and he sees everything, and when he sees things which aren't good he teaches you a lesson. But he doesn't mind really and he's only trying to help.

Lizzy

I think that Heaven is white
and you can come down to earth
whenever you want to.
And you can play games all day
and I think that all the people
like everybody there.

Katie

I think Heaven is full with clouds and God looks down on Heaven. I think good people go to Heaven and they can have a happy life and if they want to they can start there life again and be happy. If you go to Heaven you are free

I think there are flying horses
and a big big palace where God lives.
And if there's any lonely children,
God's angels look after them.

Tom

I don't want to die,
but I think when I do
I will want to.

Danny

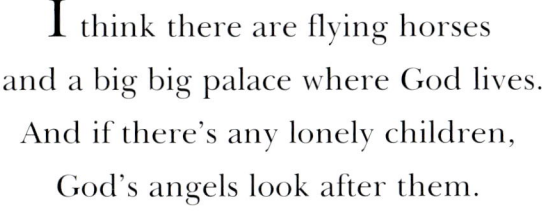

In Heaven you get fed and
looked after so you live longer.
When you go to Heaven everyone
knows that you were good.

Louise

When people go to Heaven
a bright light shines on the person
and lifts their soul into the air
and they become a star.

Paul

You can go to
all parts of your
life and do it
all over again.

Joseph

I like God.

Howard

In Heaven
everyone is kind
and they hug
each other.

Trudy

I think That Heaven is a playful place and you can decides if you wantt to Be a nor person.

I reckon that Heaven
is everywhere
because it is free
and happy.

Leanne

Heaven is a free place
and you can do whatever
you want.

Rory

God never tells you off.

Sean

In Heaven
you'll be happy.

K i r s t i e

In Heaven you can either
go back to earth
to put right your wrongs,
or stay in Heaven.

D a n i e l

I think Heaven is up
in the clouds, and when
you get to Heaven you can
stay in Heaven or have
another life.
But if you have another life,
when you are born, you
don't remember anything.

T h o m a s

I don't think Heaven is
in the sky.
I don't know where it is.
Do you know?

Julie

I think pets and other
animals go to a different
Heaven or Hell to us.
I think Heaven is high
in the clouds.
It's there but it isn't there,
if you get what I mean.

Daniel

Heaven is a playful place
and you can decide if you want
to be another person.

Hayley

Heaven is whatever you want it to be. It might be a giant park, loads of soccer pitches on clouds, or even a big, big sweet shop where you don't have to pay for anything.

Richard

In Heaven it is cloudy and you'll see everyone who has died.

Ryan

Good people go to Heaven and they can have a happy life, and if they want to they can start their life again and be happy.

Shane

In Heaven you got freedom.
  Andy

I think that when
we go to sleep
we go to visit all the
people in Heaven.
  Laura

Heaven is everywhere there are good things.
  Oliver

God is very, very big.
  Dorothy

I think Heaven is in the sky
and nice people go there
and sit down and talk
to each other.
  Jonathan

It's peaceful and
you'll make a lot of
friends in Heaven.

Kirstie

I reckon that everybody
deserves another chance.
But if you lose that chance
then it will be really lucky if
you get another chance.
I think that the homeless
should get an extra
50 years because they haven't
had much happiness
in their lives.

Lewis

In Heaven it will be happy, because, say your friend or family died, you'd go up there to be with them.
But it can also be quite sad, because up in Heaven you can look down and see people crying about your death.

Emma

The souls go around in the air. They fly around in the wind.

Nickie

You can do what you want because there is no nasty things or people to kidnap you.

Richard

You have the chance to be born on the earth again and live another life, or you can stay in Heaven.

Laura

You can have a private place all to yourself, and you could have whatever you want for free. You could sunbathe and swim in nice cool water in the lush warm sun, and then dry off under a cool palm tree in the shade.

Joseph

Up in Heaven, God and Jesus look after you,
just like they look after everyone else.

Victoria

There is always your favorite program on the television and you can watch as long as you like and then go to bed.

Ollie

It's just like down here – but it's a bit different.

Sam

Some say you go to the God
of the person who owns Jesus.
I can't remember his name.
I don't believe God made
the world because how was
he the first person who
was with the dinosaurs?
The world made itself. There
was probably a lot of fire.

N i c k i e

In Heaven you can do what you
want to do and run up and down.

L e e

I think that heaven is a place to be free.
If you go up to heaven that means that you
were good I think that your free to go anywere
no one bossys you about. The anglis look after
you in heaven

Heaven will be just like down here – only not as much trouble.

Jason

There must be a lot of people in Heaven. I hope it's not too crowded and everyone has a place to live.

Thomas

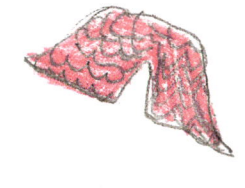

There are loads of clouds and you just lie there and you see your family.

Jody

Everyone goes to Heaven.
Anything – snakes, worms, anything
that has been killed or dies goes there.
Even Adam and Eve. Everyone.
Even tree souls.

Nickie

It's nice.
Heaven has a man called God.
You can come back to earth.
It is up high.

Jayne

People in Heaven just
hang around. They stay
where they are.

Nickie

In Heaven, people that
are blind can see and people without
any legs have got legs.

Angela

Heaven, to me, is the BEST place
you can go when you die.
Have you been good?
I hope you have, then the
angels will look after you.

Aimee

Hell

HELL CAN SEEM like a rather frightening subject to concern children with, but from their reactions they obviously have a fascination with the more gruesome aspects of the Underworld. Souls die of thirst, get imprisoned in cages, starved, whipped, boiled in lava, their lips are sewn together, their skulls get crushed, and their fingers cut off. In Hell there are spikes on the walls and bones all over the place. According to Lewis, you might get forced to clean the toilets, and can't even go round the corner without getting robbed. Aimee warns, "People who have been bad – watch out"; for, as Tracey remarks, you have only yourself to blame for ending up there.

Like the poor soul pictured bouncing himself off of a sort of trampoline into a cauldron of fire, children generally see us as assigning ourselves to the torments of Hell through our own bad actions in this life. James thinks the Devil is there to teach us a lesson at God's request. Catherine thinks the Devil is God's evil brother – echoing the heretical teachings of the early Christians known as Gnostics. Paul, however, has compassion for the Devil, who is only nasty because he didn't have any friends. Not all children believe in Hell, however. Nickie thinks everyone goes to Heaven – Hell only exists here on earth.

I think Hell is horrible,
and you don't get fed
as much as in Heaven.
In Hell you do what
you are told.

Shane

In Hell the
Devil follows
you wherever
you go.

Liam

Hell is not a very
good place to go,
because there is bad
people there.

Daniel

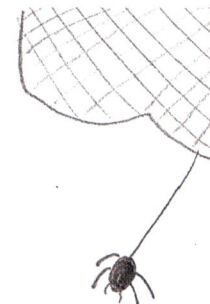

I think if you are unkind to animals you should go to Hell. Some people hit dogs and if you hit dogs, when you die you go to Hell and the Devil hits you.

Anna

I think Hell is nothing like Heaven.
It's a very bad place and I don't want to go there.

Nathan

Hell is a hot place so the souls will get dehydrated and die of thirst. People don't go to Hell straight away. They go to Heaven and God checks their record and if their records are not good, God gives them a letter and they've got to get the person's signature that they tortured or tried to kill and go back to Heaven. But if they don't get the signature they go to Hell.

Paul

Hell is deep underground. It is a dark and spooky place. People who have been bad – watch out.

Aimee

Hell is a horrible place, because you have to do things you don't really want to do.

Rachel

I think that Hell is a cold/lonly and wet place. and Hell is under the grod and ~~us~~ you can never get out of Hell and may never see your Famiy agon

Hell is a place where nobody knows.

Oliver

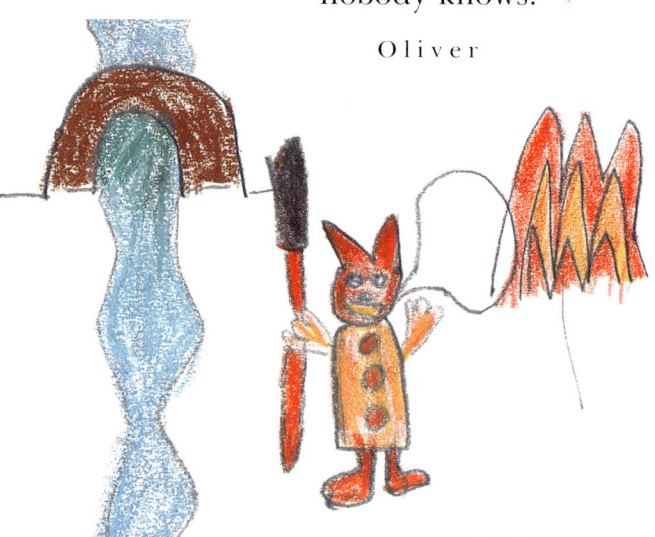

Hell is not a really nice place. They make people do horrible things like cleaning the toilet and the road. Some people can't even go round the corner without getting robbed.

Lewis

It has a man called the Devil. It has some people on rocks surrounded by lava.

Jayne

The ancient Greeks believed the dead go to the King of the Gods, Zeus. It's probably quite smart there.
I don't know.
But I think they can't see.
Zeus was actually a real person. He helped a woman get her daughter back from the Underworld.
The Underworld is probably quite dark and horrible.

Nickie

In Hell you don't get the chance to live another life, you live in torture for the rest of your life.

Laura

In Hell you forget about everyone else.

Howard

Hell is a place where you can't go anywhere – the Devil makes sure you don't go anywhere.

Sarah

If people in Hell were nice to each other, the Devil would have to let them go.

David

In Hell you have no trust with others.

Kevin

I reckon in Hell there is a master Devil who sits in a chair all the time, and if you don't do as you're told, he whips you.

Joe

I think that Hell is a cold, lonely, and wet place. And Hell is underground so you can never get out of Hell and may never see your family again.

Hayley

Only once has the lead devil come to earth. Nobody saw him, but he left strange marks in the snow. They were like a horse with two feet had left them.

Daniel

I think the Devil is nasty to us because he didn't have any friends when he was alive, so he's lonely.

John

When you die,
if you were evil in life
you go to Hell.
If you were not too bad
you are sent back to
earth to help someone
or put right a problem.
If you do it right,
you can go to Heaven.

Danie

If the Devil gets them
and burns their souls,
they just fall asleep.

Jason

In Hell they treat
you like you're nobody.

Stacey

After you die,
you can't feel.

Nickie

If I went to Hell I'd try and escape by digging a tunnel up to Heaven. But the devils would probably catch me because they are clever.

Jane

I think god gives you two chances but on your 3rd you go to hell or have bad luck... In hell you are slaves or put into a cage!!

Most people that go to Hell get starved and have a ball around their leg. Some people go on trial. If they behave themselves they go to Heaven.

Oliver

I n Hell they cut
your head off
and then it grows
again and then they
cut it off again.

Fran

I think that Hell is a red
dark cave underground.
I think the head devil is
God's evil brother.

Catherine

I wish the Devil
was not so horrid,
but that's his job
so he has got to be.

Jacob

You're not allowed
to talk and if you do, they
sew your lips together.

Richard

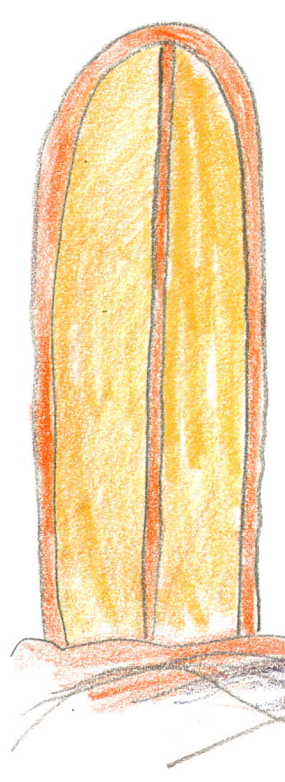

There is a gate and dark black stairs, and as you walk down there is a person in a cage with fire spitting up at the bottom and the Devil is laughing.

Jonathan

If you go to Hell, God tells the Devil to teach you a lesson.

James

In Hell,
nothing happens.
It is very very boring.

Jake

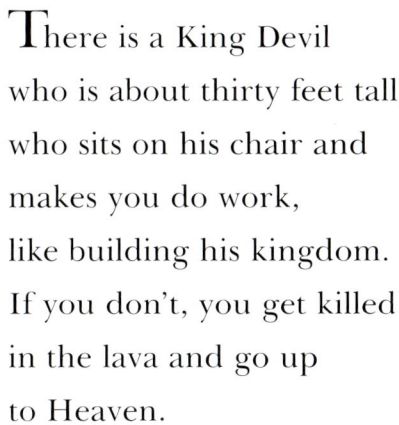

Hell is an evil place
where you are miserable
all the time.

Kirstie

There is a King Devil
who is about thirty feet tall,
who sits on his chair and
makes you do work,
like building his kingdom.
If you don't, you get killed
in the lava and go up
to Heaven.

Jason

Hell is like a bad dream.
Josie

I think Hell is far, far away – so nobody can see it.
Hollie

When you go to Hell you stay there until you say you're sorry, and then you can go to Heaven or come back to earth to be a good person.
William

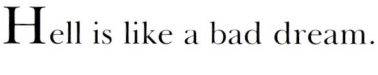

I think that Hell is horrible and nobody speaks to you.

Ben

I wish everyone would go to Heaven and nobody had to be tortured in Hell.

Jeffrey

Hell is a place with red mud and with stuff falling from the top. I would say it was in the middle of the earth. I think people can't move and the Devil does something to them to stop them moving.

Ashley

There is a man who decides
who goes to Heaven and who goes
to Hell and sometimes he gets it
wrong and everyone is very angry.
And the man who went to Heaven
by mistake tries to hide
so he doesn't have to go to Hell.

Tony

The Devil has big teeth and he's
always trying to frighten you, but if
you aren't frightened, he lets you go.

Rick

1. in hell it is hot.
2. hell is bad
3. it is below Heaven
4. it has a man too called the Devil.
5. it has some people on Rocks
6. surrounded by Laver.

I don't think children should go to Hell because it's not fair.

Julie

Sometimes God goes to Hell and rescues people. They are very lucky and they like him very much.

Henry

Hell is sad.

Kirstie

When you die you
go in a yard with
people with other
people's bodies.

Jonathan

In Hell no one
has any money
and everyone
is very poor and
they don't like it.

George

You walk into this black room and
then into a red room and here there
is loads of fire, and if you don't do
what you are told, you get burned
or turned into a devil.

Stacy

The Devil sets a time and when the alarm clock goes off, they cut a rope and you fall in the lava.

Sadie

In hell you have a bad life and a unhappy life. In hell you have notrust with others.

In Hell you aren't allowed to see anyone, so you don't make friends.

Hollie

I think if you haven't believed in anything, that would not be good. It would be just terrible. It would be like you hadn't got anything to eat. That's Hell.

Nickie

If you're bad the Devil crushes your skull.

Jody

If you go to Hell, they chop your fingers off if you do something wrong.

Craig

In Hell if you go into a corner, you ain't got no way out.

Sadie

In Hell all the people want to come back and say sorry, and tell their friends not to be bad.

Noel

There is no Hell after death. Just before death. After it's brilliant.

Nickie

Sometimes bad people are let out of Hell and go to Heaven because Jesus feels sorry for them.

Jenny